••○ *BULLETPOINTS* ○••

CARS & BIKES

Sean Connolly and John Farndon
Consultant: Brian Williams

Miles Kelly
PUBLISHING

First published in 2004 by Miles Kelly Publishing Ltd
Bardfield Centre, Great Bardfield
Essex, CM7 4SL

2 4 6 8 10 9 7 5 3 1

Editor: Isla MacCuish

Design: WhiteLight

Picture Research: Liberty Newton

Production: Estela Godoy

British Library Cataloguing-in-Publication Data
A catalogue record for this book is available from the British Library

ISBN 1-84236-375-1

Printed in China

www.mileskelly.net
info@mileskelly.net

J759,697
£6

The publishers would like to thank the following artists who have contributed to this book:
Nicholas Forder, Peter Gregory, Gary Hincks, Janos Marffy, Terry Riley,
Peter Sarson, Guy Smith, Mike White

Contents

The Benz

- **Karl Benz (1844–1929)** and his wife Berta were the German creators of the first successful petrol-driven car in 1885.

- **At the age of 16** before Lenoir built his petrol-powered cart, Karl Benz dreamed of 'a unit that could supplant the steam engine'.

- **Karl and Berta Benz** began developing their car in the 1870s, while trying to earn money from a tin-making business. By 1880 they were so penniless they could barely afford to eat every day.

▼ *The Benz tricycle was the world's first successful petrol-driven car.*

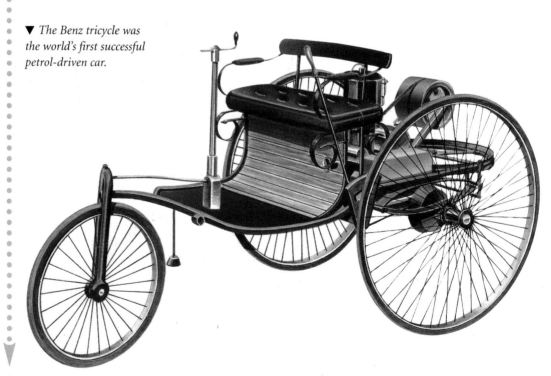

- **Their first car** was a small tricycle, but had a water-cooled four-stroke engine with electric ignition.

- **Karl Benz** tested the car round the streets of their home town of Mannheim after dark to avoid scaring people.

- **Berta Benz** recharged the car's battery after each trip by pedalling a dynamo attached to her sewing machine.

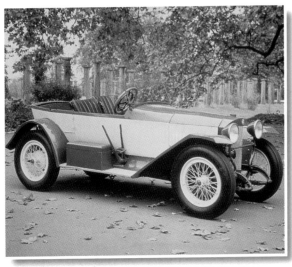

▲ *A Benz automobile from 1925.*

- **Berta Benz** secretly made the first long, 100 km journey in the car, without Karl knowing. On the journey to her home in Pforzheim, she had to clear the fuel-line with a hairpin and use her garters to cure an electrical short.

- **The Benz** caused a stir when shown at the Paris World Fair in 1889.

- **Backed by F. von Fischer** and Julian Ganss, Benz began making his cars for sale in 1889 – the first cars ever made for sale.

- **By 1900** Benz was making over 600 cars a year.

Model T Ford

◀ *Ford cars are still among the most popular on sale today.*

- **In 1905** most cars were 'coach-built' which meant they were individually built by hand. This made them costly toys available only to the rich.

- **The dream of Detroit farmboy** Henry Ford was to make 'a motor car for the great multitude – a car so low in price that no man making a good fortune will be unable to own one.'

- **Ford's solution** was to make a car, which he called the Model T, using a mass-production technique.

- **Mass production** meant using huge teams of men, each adding a small part to the car as it moved along the production line.

- **Body-panels** for the Model T were stamped out by machines, not hammered by hand as with earlier cars.

- **In 1908** when Ford launched the Model T, fewer than 200,000 people in the USA owned cars.

- **In 1913** 250,000 people owned Model Ts alone.

- **By 1930** 15 million Model Ts had been sold.

- **One of the keys to the T** was standardizations. Ford said early Ts were available in 'any colour they like so long as it's black'. Later models came in other colours.

- **The T's fragile-looking chassis** earned it the nickname 'Tin Lizzie', but it was made of tough vanadium steel.

▲ *The tough, cheap and reliable Model T – the first mass-produced car – put America on the road for the first time and earned the affection of two generations of American families.*

Early cars

- **In 1890** Frenchman Emile Levassor made the first real car, with an engine at the front. He laughed, saying, 'C'est brutal, mais ca marche' ('It's rough, but it goes').

- **The Duryea** brothers made the first successful American car in 1893.

- **Early accidents** made cars seem dangerous. Until 1896 in Britain and 1901 in New York cars had to be preceded by a man on foot waving a red flag.

- **In 1895** the French Panhard-Levassor company made the first covered 'saloon' car.

- **In 1898** Renault drove the wheels with a shaft not a chain.

- **The Oldsmobile** Curved Dash of 1900 was the first car to sell in thousands.

- **On early cars** speed was controlled by moving a small ignition advance lever backwards or forwards.

▼ *Frederick Lanchester designed some of the world's earliest motor-cars. He built his first automobile in 1896.*

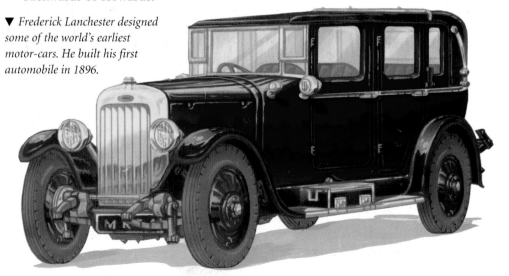

▲ *By 1904, many cars were starting to have the familiar layout of cars today – engine at the front, driver on one side, steering wheel, petrol tank at the back, a shaft to drive the wheels and so on.*

- **Dirt roads**, oil spray and noise meant early motorists needed protective clothing such as goggles.

- **The first cars** had wooden or wire-spoked wheels. Pressed-steel wheels like today's came in after 1945.

- **In 1906** an American steam-driven car, the Stanley Steamer, broke the Land Speed Record at over 205 km/h.

Luxury cars

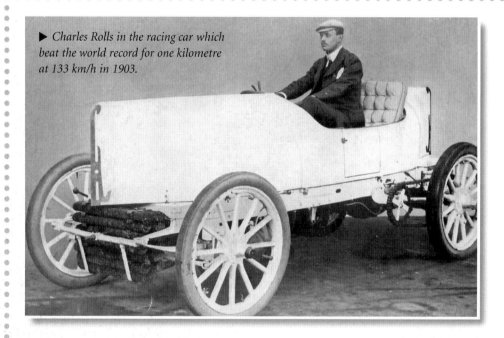

▶ *Charles Rolls in the racing car which beat the world record for one kilometre at 133 km/h in 1903.*

- **The first Rolls-Royce** was made by Charles Rolls and Henry Royce. It was known as the 'best car in the world'.

- **The Rolls-Royce Silver Ghost** got its name for its ghost-like quietness and shiny aluminium body.

- **Today** each Rolls-Royce takes three months to build.

- **The winged girl** statuette on the bonnet of a Rolls-Royce is called 'Spirit of Ecstasy' and dates from 1911.

- **In the 1930s** Ettore Bugatti set out to build the best car ever with the Bugatti Royale. Only six were built, and they are now the world's most valuable cars.

- **The name Royale** comes from the King of Spain, Alfonso XIII, who was to buy the first model.

- **In 1925** drinks-maker André Dubonnet had a special version of the Hispano-Suiza H6B built with a body made entirely of tulipwood.

- **In the 1930s** American car-makers like Cord, Auburn and Packard made magnificent cars that Hollywood stars posed beside and Chicago gangsters drove.

- **Every 1934** Auburn speedster was sold with a plaque certifying it had been driven at over 160 km/h by racing driver Ab Jenkins.

- **The Mercedes in** Mercedes-Benz was the name of the daughter of Emil Jellinek, who sold the cars in the USA.

▶ *Bentley is one of the great names in luxury cars. But founder Owen Bentley believed in racing as advertisement. The Bentley name gained lasting fame with success in the Le Mans 24-hour races of the 1920s. This is a 1950s rally entry.*

People's cars

▲ *The 1959 Mini, designed by Alec Issigonis, set a trend in small-car design, with the engine mounted across the car driving the front wheels.*

- **The first car** for ordinary people was Ford's Model T Ford built their 10 millionth car in 1924 and their 50 millionth in 1959.

- **The USA** began making more than a million cars a year in 1916, of which over a third were Model Ts. No other country made one million cars a year until the UK in 1954.

- **Ford US** introduced weekly payment plans for new cars in 1923. The Nazis later borrowed the idea for the VW Beetle.

- **The Model A Ford** sold one million within 14 months of its launch in December 1927. The Ford Escort of 1980 sold a million in just 11 months.

- **The French Citroën 2CV** was designed to carry 'a farmer in a top hat across a ploughed field without breaking the eggs on the seat beside him'.

- **The VW Beetle** was the brainchild of the Nazi dictator Adolf Hitler who wanted a cheap car to be available for all Germans. It was created in 1938 by Ferdinand Porsche.

- **The war interrupted** VW Beetle production when it had barely begun, but it was resumed after the war.

- **The 10 millionth** VW Beetle was built in 1965. Over 22 million have now been sold.

- **The Soviet-built Lada**, based on a design by Fiat, was one of the most inexpensive cars ever.

- **The first British car** to sell a million was the Morris Minor, between 1949 and 1962.

▲ *The German Volkswagen Beetle was first driven in 1938. A new-look design came out in 1998.*

Supercars

◀ *The Porsche 911 is one of the classic supercars, first introduced in 1964, but still looking sleek many years later.*

● **The Mercedes Benz 300SL** of 1952 was one of the first supercars of the post-war years, famous for its stylish flip-up 'Gullwing' doors.

● **The Jaguar E-type** was the star car of the early 1960s with incredibly sleek lines and 250 km/h performance.

● **The Ford Mustang** was one of the first young and lively 'pony' cars, introduced in 1964.

● **The Aston Martin DB6** was the classic supercar of the late 1960s, driven by film spy James Bond.

● **The Porsche 911 turbo** was the fastest accelerating production car for almost twenty years after its launch in 1975, scorching from 0 to 100 km/h in just 5.4 seconds.

- **The Lamborghini** Countach was the fastest supercar of the 1970s and 1980s, with a top speed of 295 km/h.
- **The Maclaren F1** can accelerate from 0 to 160 km/h in less time than it takes to read this sentence.
- **The Maclaren F1** is capable of going from 0 to 160 km/h and back to 0 again in under 20 seconds.
- **A tuned version** of the Chevrolet Corvette, the Callaway Sledge Hammer, can hit over 400 km/h.

> ...**FASCINATING FACT**...
> The Ford GT-90 has a top speed of
> 378 km/h and zooms from 0 to 100 km/h
> in 3.2 seconds.

▲ *Mercedes wins the Fomula One World Championship in 1954.*

Record-breaking cars

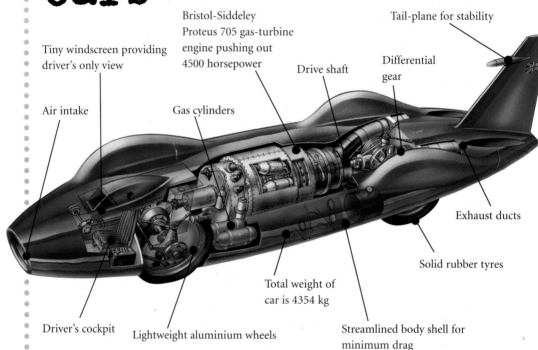

Tiny windscreen providing driver's only view

Bristol-Siddeley Proteus 705 gas-turbine engine pushing out 4500 horsepower

Tail-plane for stability

Drive shaft

Differential gear

Air intake

Gas cylinders

Exhaust ducts

Solid rubber tyres

Total weight of car is 4354 kg

Driver's cockpit

Lightweight aluminium wheels

Streamlined body shell for minimum drag

▲ *Donald Campbell took on the record-breaking mantle of his father – and the Bluebird name for his car. On 17 July 1964, Campbell's Bluebird hit a world record 690.909 km/h on the salt flats at Lake Eyre in South Australia. At one moment he hit over 716 km/h – faster than any wheel-driven car has ever been.*

- **The first car speed record** was achieved by an electric Jentaud car in 1898 at Acheres near Paris. Driven by the Comte de Chasseloup-Laubat, the car hit 63.14 km/h. Camille Jenatzy vied with de Chasseloup-Laubat for the record, raising it to 105.85 km/h in his car *Jamais Contente* in 1899.

- **Daytona Beach** in Florida became a venue for speed trials in 1903.

- **The biggest engine** ever to be raced in a Grand Prix was the 19,891 cc V4 of American Walter Christie, which he entered in the 1907 French Grand Prix. Later the Christie was the first front-wheel-drive car to win a major race – a 400 km race on Daytona Beach.

- **The record** for the circuit at Brooklands in England was set in 1935 by John Cobb in a Napier-Railton at 1 min 0.41 sec 230.79 km/h and never beaten.

- **In 1911** the governing body for the Land Speed Record said that cars had to make two runs in opposite directions over a 1 km course to get the record.

- **In 1924** Sir Malcolm Campbell broke the Land Speed Record for the first of many times in a Sunbeam at 235.17 km/h. In 1925 he hit 242 km/h for the first time. But his most famous record-breaking runs were in the 1930s in his own *Bluebird* cars.

- **In 1947** John Cobb drove with tremendous skill to reach 634.27 km/h in his Railton-Mobil. This stood as the record for 17 years.

- **In 1964** the rules were changed to allow jet and rocket-propelled cars to challenge for the Land Speed Record. The next year Craig Breedlove drove his three-wheeler jet *Spirit of America* to over 846.78 km/h.

- **In 1970** Gary Gabelich set the record over 1000 km/h with his rocket-powered *Blue Flame*. This record wasn't beaten until Richard Noble roared to 1019.37 km/h in his Rolls-Royce jet-powered *Thrust 2* in 1983.

Racing cars

- **The first recorded motor race** was in France in 1894, between Paris and Rouen, and was won jointly by a Peugeot and a Panhard, after a faster steam-tractor was disqualified.

- **In 1903 a 12.9 litre,** 90hp Renault won the first Le Mans Grand Prix two-day race, averaging 104.95 km/h, and sometimes reaching 160 km/h.

- **An American Duesenberg** won the 1921 Le Mans, a streamlined racer powered by a 3 litre, straight-eight engine, and the first Grand Prix car to use hydraulic brakes.

- **Throughout the 1920s,** lightweight, easily controlled Bugattis dominated the rugged Targa Florio race through the mountains of Sicily, outperforming their heavier, more powerful rivals.

- **In 1948 the Maserati company** began to use tubular chassis frames for its Formula 1, supercharged cars, which were successfully raced by champion drivers such as Argentinian Juan Fangio.

- **The Tipo '500' Ferrari** dominated Formula Two racing in the early 1950s, especially when driven by Alberto Ascari, and Ferraris won 30 out of 33 races entered in 1952-1953.

- **The Indianapolis 500** is America's most famous race, in which the cars battle around a 4 km oval track for 804 km, at speeds close to and sometimes under 40 seconds per lap.

- **Pioneered by cars** such as the Lotus-Cosworth 78 and 79, racers in the late 1970s used special aerodynamic shapes to suck the car chassis downwards, increasing tyre-grip.

- **The tyres of a Formula One car** were only 5 inches wide in the mid-1960s, but by the early 1980s a maximum width of 18 inches had been set.

18

- **Formula One motor racing** is the world's most expensive sport, and it costs £20 million or more a year for a team to compete.

▲ *In 1928, Bentley drivers W. Barnato and B. Rubin won the Le Mans 24 Hours with an average speed of just 111 km/h.*

Gears

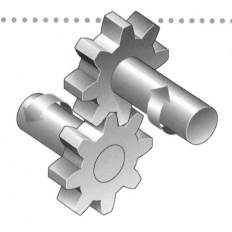

▲ *Simple cogs reverse direction of rotation.*

▼ *Bevels move direction of rotation through a right angle.*

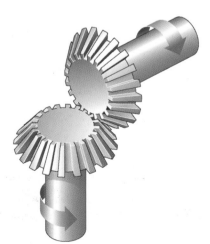

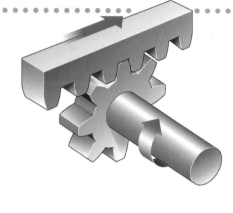

▲ *Rack and pinion changes rotation to sliding motion.*

▼ *Worm gears turn fast rotation into slower, stronger rotation at right angles.*

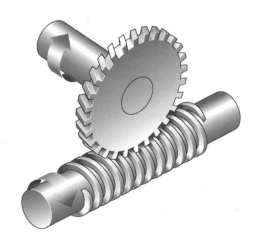

▶ *Gears are used in a huge range of machines, from watches to motorbikes, for transmitting movement from one shaft to another.*

- **Gears** are pairs of toothed wheels that interlock and so transmit power from one shaft to another.

- **The first gears** were wooden, with wooden teeth. By the 6th century AD, wooden gears of all kinds were used in windmills, watermills and winches.

- **Metal gears** appeared in 87BC and were later used for clocks. Today, all gears are metal and made on a 'gear-hobbing' machine.

- **Simple gears** are wheels with straight-cut teeth.

- **Helical gears** have slanting rather than straight teeth, and run smoother. The gears in cars are helical.

- **Bevel or mitre gears** are cone-shaped, allowing the gear shafts to interlock at right angles.

- **In worm gears** one big helical gear interlocks with a long spiral gear on a shaft at right angles.

- **Planetary gears** have a number of gear wheels known as spurs or planets that rotate around a central 'sun' gear.

J159,697

- **In a planetary gear** the planet and sun gear all rotate within a ring called an annulus.

...**FASCINATING FACT**...
Automatic gearboxes in cars use planetary or epicyclic gears.

21

Bicycles

▲ *Bicycles are the cheapest, most reliable form of transport ever, and in the 1920s many tradesmen adapted them for use.*

- **The first bicycle** was the 1818 'draisienne' of Baron de Drais. The rider scooted his feet on the ground to move.

- **In 1839** Scots blacksmith Kirkpatrick Macmillan invented the first bicycle with pedals and brakes.

- **On Macmillan's velocipede** pedals were linked by rods to cranks on the back wheel. These turned the wheel slowly.

- **In 1861** French father and son Pierre and Ernest Michaux stuck the pedals directly on the front wheel to make the first successful bicycle, nicknamed 'boneshaker'.

- **In 1870** James Starley improved the boneshaker with the Ordinary. A huge front wheel gave high speed with little pedalling.

- **In 1874** H. J. Lawson made the first chain-driven bicycle. This was called a 'safety bicycle' because it was safer than the tall Ordinary.
- **In 1885** Starley's nephew John made the Rover Safety bicycle. Air-filled tyres were added in 1890, and the modern bicycle was born.
- **By 1895** four million Americans were riding bicycles.
- **Today** 50 million people in the USA cycle regularly.
- **More people** in China cycle today than in the rest of the world put together.

▼ *Bicycle-riding has grown in popularity and many cities have established special lanes for cyclists in parks and along streets.*

Motorbikes

- **The first petrol engine** motorbike was built by Gottlieb Daimler in Germany in 1885.

- **Most small motorbikes** have a two-stroke petrol engine, typically air-cooled and quite noisy.

- **Most larger motorbikes** have four-stroke petrol engines, which typically are water-cooled.

- **On most bikes** the engine drives the rear wheel through a chain; on some the drive is through a shaft.

- **A trail bike** is a bike with a high mounted frame and chunky tyres, designed to be ridden over rough tracks.

- **Motorbikes** with engines smaller than 50cc may be called mopeds, because in the past they had pedals as well as an engine.

FN·5679

◄ *Many enthusiasts still ride motorbikes like this from the 1930s when motorcycling was in its heyday.*

24

▲ *The rider of a superbike crouches as low as possible over the handlebars to minimize wind resistance.*

- **The biggest motorbikes** have engines of around 1200cc.

- **The most famous** motorbike race in the world is the Isle of Man TT, or Tourist Trophy.

- **In speedway,** bikes with no brakes or gears are raced round dirt tracks.

Racing bikes

- **In the 1911 Senior TT** (Tourist Trophy) race on the Isle of Man's Mountain circuit, Indian racers from the USA took first, second and third places, all with English riders.

- **The first USA motorbike races** were held at the turn of the 20th century on banked wooden circuits. The first bike to average 160 km/h for a lap was a 'Big Valve' Excelsior, in 1912.

- **In 1916 Indian introduced** the Model H racer, which raced with great success on board and dirt tracks, and could exceed 193 km/h.

- **The first foreign rider** to win a TT was an Italian, Omobono Tenni, riding a Moto Guzzi racing bike to win the Lightweight TT in 1937.

- **The Moto Guzzi V8 racer,** with an estimated top speed of 252 km/h, was far too fast and powerful for the race tracks of the mid-1950s, and the international racing authorities banned it from competition.

- **Without brakes or gears,** speedway bikes, which are 500cc and single cylinder, with spindly, bicycle-type frames, compete in short sprint races around oval shale tracks.

- **After World War ll,** all American race bikes had to be based on high-volume production machines, and Harley-Davidson brought out the WR 750cc Flathead to conform to the new rules.

- **In the late 40s and early 50s,** single-cylinder Manx Norton bikes took most places across the board at the 321-km Blue Riband Championships at the Daytona Beach circuit in the USA.

- **A trio of BSA Rocket 3s,** with triple cylinders, 740cc engines and ultra-light frames took 1st, 2nd and third places at the 1971 Daytona 321-km event.

- **Ducati's M900 Monster production bike,** first seen in 1993, had a V-twin engine and a top speed of 193 km/h, and gave birth in 1995 to the CH Racing Azzalini version, of which only 20 were built.

▲ *Triumph T595 Daytona. This 1200cc machine produces over 140 bhp. It was released in 1993. This model dates from 1997.*

Classic bikes

- **The first Indian motorbike** had a single cylinder and appeared in the USA in 1901. The 600cc Indian Scout won many prizes as a production racer between 1920 and 1931.

- **The Harley Davidson WLA** had a 750cc V-twin engine and was used extensively in World War ll – the US Army alone bought over 60,000 of them for messenger, convoy and police duties.

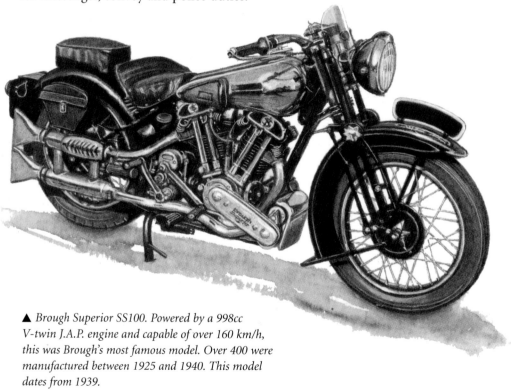

▲ *Brough Superior SS100. Powered by a 998cc V-twin J.A.P. engine and capable of over 160 km/h, this was Brough's most famous model. Over 400 were manufactured between 1925 and 1940. This model dates from 1939.*

- **Often referred to as the Rolls Royce** of motorbikes, the 1000cc Brough Superior SS100, introduced in 1925 had a guaranteed top speed of 160 km/h. Lawrence of Arabia owned at least six of them.

- **The 1930 Ariel Square Four** was a 500cc luxury performance bike built to appeal to a wide audience, and reappeared in 1937 as the Model 4G, with a 995cc, overhead valve engine.

- **Appearing in 1937, the Triumph Speed Twin** could cruise effortlessly for hours at 96 km/h, and had a top speed of 144 km/h, all for about £75.

- **Elvis Presley owned a Harley-Davidson Electra Glide,** the ultimate American cruising machine, designed for comfort, with a 1340cc V-twin engine, and weighing a massive 800lbs.

- **The Norton Dominator of 1952** was a production tourer built onto Norton's revolutionary Featherbed racing frame. By 1962 it had a 647cc engine and a top speed of 180 km/h.

- **The Honda CB750,** first appearing in 1969, was the first of the Superbikes, with its 4-cylinder, 750cc engine, and spearheaded the Japanese 'invasion' which overwhelmed the British bike industry.

- **The 1992 Honda Fireblade CBR 900** was light, responsive, and incredibly fast, and quickly became Britain's best selling sports bike, with its 918cc water-cooled engine giving a top speed of 257 km/h.

- **The Ducati 916** combined brilliant space-age design with high-speed performance when it was previewed at the 1993 Milan Show. It could cover 400 m from a standing start in 10.7 seconds.

Trucks

- **Trucks or lorries** can weigh 40 tonnes or more – maybe as much as 50 cars.

- **Cars** are are normally powered by petrol engines; trucks are typically powered by diesel engines.

- **Cars** typically have five forward gears; trucks often have as many as 16.

- **Cars** typically have four wheels. Trucks often have 12 or 16 to help spread the weight of the loads they need to carry.

- **Many trucks** have the same basic cab and chassis (the framework supporting the body). Different bodies are fitted on to the chassis to suit the load.

 ▲ Huge trucks transport heavy machinery used for farming and building.

▲ *Many trucks are fitted with refrigeration sytems. This means they can carry huge loads of perishable goods, such as food, over long distances.*

- **Some trucks** are constructed in two parts, hinged at the join. These are called articulated trucks.

- **The cab and engine** of an articulated truck is called the tractor unit. The load is carried in the trailer.

- **In Australia** one tractor may pull several trailers in a 'road-train' along the long, straight desert roads.

- **The longest truck** is the Arctic Snow Train, first made for the US army. This is 174 m long and has 54 wheels.

- **Large trucks** are sometimes called 'juggernauts'. Juggernaut was a form of the Hindu god Vishnu who rode a huge chariot, supposed by Europeans to crush people beneath its wheels.

31

Buses and coaches

▲ *Like most early buses, this one from the early 1920s was built by adding a coach body to a lorry base.*

- **Horse-drawn stagecoaches** were the first regular public coach services between two or more points or 'stages'. They were first used in London during the 1630s.

- **Stagecoaches** reached their heyday in the early 1800s when new tarred roads made travel faster. Coaches went from London to Edinburgh in 40 hours.

- **Bus is short** for 'omnibus' which means 'for all' in latin. The word first came into use in Paris in the 1820s for big coaches carrying lots of people on shorter, local journeys.

- **In 1830** Goldsworthy Gurney put a steam engine in a coach to make the first powered bus. It operated four times a day between Cheltenham and Gloucester in England.

- **In the 1850s** British government laws restricted steam road vehicles, so big new cities developed horse buses.

- **In 1895** a petrol-engined bus was built in Germany.

- **In 1904** the London General Omnibus Co. ran the first petrol-engined bus services. The buses were double-decked.

- **In 1905** the first motor buses ran on New York's 5th Avenue.

- **In 1928** the first transcontinental bus service crossed the USA.

- **From the 1950s** articulated buses were used in European cities. A trailer joined to the bus carries extra passengers.

◀ *Stagecoaches carried passengers, luggage and mail over long distances.*

Trams and cable cars

- **Trams** are buses that run on rails laid through city streets. They are called streetcars in the USA.

- **Early trams** in the 1830s were pulled by horses. By the 1870s, horse-drawn trams were used in many cities.

- **In 1834** Thomas Davenport, a blacksmith from Vermont, USA built a battery-powered electric tram.

- **In 1860** an American called George Train set up battery-powered electric tram systems in London.

▶ *The original Hallidie cable car system dating from 1873 still runs in San Francisco.*

▶ *Some cable cars are used as ski lifts. They run on cables suspended between towers.*

- **In 1873** Andrew Hallidie introduced cable cars in San Francisco. The cars were hauled by a cable running in a slot in the street. A powerhouse pulled the cable at a speed of 14 km/h. Similar systems were built in many cities in the 1880s but were soon replaced by electric trams.

- **In 1888** Frank Sprague demonstrated a tram run from electric overhead cables in Richmond in the USA.

- **In most US trams,** electric current was picked up via a long pole with a small wheel called a shoe that slid along the cable. The pick-up was called a trolley. Many European trams, however, picked up current via a collapsible frame called a pantograph.

- **In the early 1900s,** electric tram systems were set up in most world cities.

- **In the 1930s** most cities, except in eastern Europe and Russia, replaced trams with buses.

- **In the 1990s** some cities, like Manchester in England, built new tramways, because they are fume-free.

Moving on snow

- **Vehicles** designed to move on snow are supported on flat boards called runners, skids or skis. These slide over snow easily and spread the vehicle's weight over a larger area.

- **Sleds or sleighs** drawn by horses or dogs may have been the first vehicles ever used by humans.

- **Cutters** are light, graceful horse-drawn sleighs first introduced in the USA about 1800.

- **Troikas** are Russian sleighs (or carriages) drawn by three horses. The middle horse is supposed to trot while the outer horses gallop in particular ways.

▲ *Cutters are still used in the north-eastern USA as a charming way of getting around in the winter snows.*

▶ *A skidoo is a motorized sled driven on snowy surfaces.*

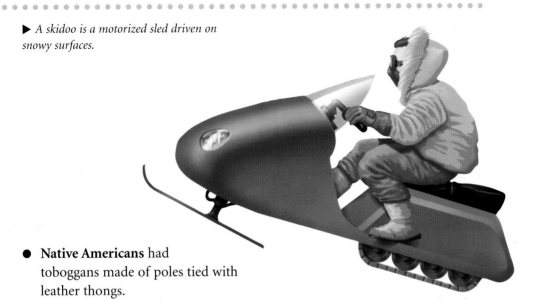

- **Native Americans** had toboggans made of poles tied with leather thongs.

- **Snowmobiles** are vehicles with two skis at the front and a motor-driven track roll at the back. Racing snowmobiles can reach over 160 km/h.

- **Snowmobiles** are steered by handlebars that control the skis and by the shifting of the driver's weight.

- **The first propeller-driven** snowmobile was built in the 1920s. Tracked snowmobiles were developed in 1959 by Canadian Joseph Bombardier.

- **In the 1960s** carved wooden skis dating back 8000 years were found in a bog at Vis near the Urals in Russia.

- **The earliest skates** were mostly small bone skis tied to the feet.

Tractors

- **Tractors** are motor vehicles used mostly on farms for pulling or pushing machines such as ploughs.

- **Tractors** are also used in factories, by the army, for heavy jobs like logging and for clearing snow.

▲ *An early Fordson tractor made in 1917.*

▲ *Modern tractors can be adapted to operate all kinds of devices, including this haybailer, via the power take-off.*

- **Steam-powered tractors** called 'traction engines' were introduced in 1834 by Walter Hancock.

- **Traction-engines** could pull up to 40 ploughs at once via long chains, but they were too cumbersome to be practical in hilly country.

- **Petrol-powered tractors** were introduced in the 1890s but they were not powerful enough for most farm work.

- **The first all-purpose** farm tractors appeared in the 1920s and soon began to replace horses and oxen.

- **Ploughs and other equipment** are drawn along via the drawbar on the back of the tractor.

- **The power take-off** or PTO allows the tractor's engine to power equipment such as potato diggers.

- **Twenty-five percent of all tractors** are in the USA.

Index